THE WORLD NEEDS MORE BELLY RUBS

MARK VINCENT LINCIR

Edited by Kayla Peek

Back cover photo by Scatter Blue Media LLC

Published by Leftback Publishing LLC

PMB 501

835 W. Warner Road, Suite 101

Gilbert, AZ 85233

ISBN-13: 9780985127213

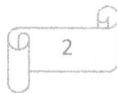

Also by Mark Vincent Lincir

A SOCCER LIFE IN SHORTS

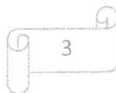

INTRODUCTION

He eats, he sleeps and he goes for walks. Those are all things he likes but I don't think he would tell you that he actually *needs* them. The one thing that is a requirement in his life...is a belly rub.

Our dog Durden has a passion/borderline obsession with belly rubs. He doesn't return the favor because he can't. But even if he could I don't think he would because he would ration that if there was more time for belly rubs *HE* should be the recipient.

Don't get me wrong...he is an awesome dog and we love him. He keeps his life simple, yet enjoyable and his biggest extravagance is the belly rub. I'm sure in his head he has devised a machine that he can walk up to and bump a switch with his paw to enjoy belly rubs 24/7 if he so pleases.

Unfortunately, he never took engineering classes in school and doesn't have a very wealthy group of friends that he could tap for seed money. Nevertheless, he loves his life as long as it involves belly rubs. And we try to accommodate him as much as we can. If he owned a car his bumper sticker would read, "It's always a good time for a belly rub."

He...oops, I mean we, have a nightly ritual. I usually give him a belly rub as we all watch television before going to bed. Then, when I go to brush my teeth low and behold who walks in our bedroom door...

Durden...for one more belly rub.

He lies down behind me on the carpet while I rinse the toothpaste out of my mouth. As I turn to him he instinctively rolls over and prepares himself for his second belly rub of the evening (this is all within ten minutes of each other). After that I pat his stomach gently to let him know it's over and prepare myself for bed. He leaves the room somewhat content, but never totally satisfied (the belly rub did *stop* after all).

I admire his commitment to tradition and spontaneity (he will gladly accept a belly rub at *any time*, even if he is in a meeting)...and most of all the simplicity of his happiness. You can take away a lot from him and he'd probably adapt without a problem.

But try to deny him belly rubs and there will be a problem! Find a simple pleasure that keeps you going day in and day out and *make* time to enjoy it. It's when you are happy that you can help inspire those around you to find happiness in their days as well.

Happiness is contagious and should be shared. If Durden could talk, he would tell us all that we all need more belly rubs...and that nine out of 10 doctors surveyed say that a few belly rubs a day makes everything better. He'd be fibbing about the doctor part, but he is living proof of the fact that it makes everything better.

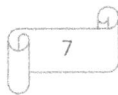

ACE IN THE HOLE

A smile.

A frown.

Turn your world upside down.

No rules.

No assumptions.

Real love only for those with gumption.

Dance around it all you want.

Your humor is what you should flaunt.

If there's nothing left.

Head out the exit door.

Pick your pride up off the floor.

BAILED

The cold cuts through his bleached hair like a crisp arrow.

His eyes spy the door, they get narrow.

Nerves of steel don't matter in situations like this.

No time for indecision, no dreaming of bliss.

He steps quietly and begins to knock.

The clock goes tick-tock.

The wind stops, the rain subsides.

The memories of their time together glide.

A lock is undone, the door cracks.

It's not her, she's gone.

No tracks.

Just gone into the world.

Coming back not too soon.

Leave her alone, you acted like a baboon!

Giving up will be harder said than done,

But she deserves to be in charge of letting her own life come undone.

AN IRONIC SYMPHONY

Leaves falling.

Waves crashing.

Sounds carrying.

Across windswept plains.

And white-capped oceans.

A friendship carved from birth.

Conversations over pre-dawn coffee.

A three-legged dog that can talk but can't listen.

A car that flies with the help of Dumbo.

A gigantic bowl of soup that you can swim in.

Heartache, heartbreak.

Laughing at yourself at the most inopportune time.

ES ZIDIO

Sun-drenched sunsets.

Fast speedy cars.

Talkative people who hog conversations.

Dark, lightless corners.

Hopeful optimists.

The obvious and beautiful.

Simple, uncluttered, and slightly redundant.

Original...

OPTIMISM REIGNS

The night sits still.

But my mind infinitely races.

From joy and love to tears and fear.

Happy that my love is near.

Morning will be here quicker than I know.

And thank God there will be at least one more day to go.

ESCAPE IT

Waves of worry crashing on your head.

Making your brain feel like it's full of lead.

Gotta go and clear it, find some relief.

No good holding in all that grief.

Life is too short to get caught up in all the drama.

Take a ride off into the sunset on an egotistical llama.

THE MIGHTY TAN

The face is creased, uneven and tan.

The markings of a sun-obsessed man.

Being outside is the only way to live.

Only stay inside if there is nothing left to give.

It was always the beach, pool or hills.

No business living life looking out window sills.

From daybreak until sunset it pulled him close.

Nothing wrong with living life to the most!

GUTS

You want to ask her.

But you want to wait.

The winner does not go to those who hesitate.

Put it out there, give it a shot.

Don't let your life or ego rot.

Taking risks is what it's all about.

No pain, no gain, nothing to tout.

Who cares if she says no?

You're still alive!

If you're too embarrassed you might break out into hives.

But you can say you did it.

You took your chance.

Maybe it'll even get you to the big dance.

WASHOUT

Clouds racing through the midday sun.

Messing up your work that you're trying to get done.

Then the rain comes and you have to stop.

Work any longer and you might just drop.

For today is a rainout.

Go home and relax.

Get back to that hobby, your nap, your tax.

It's not every day that your day gets cuts due to nature.

It's a sign that we need to slow down.

Turn it all off and close your eyes to the world.

Let yourself spin off to the magical, even the absurd.

Have a great dream before morning comes and you have to do it all again.

And don't forget to give credit to the rain for being there, for being your friend.

BETRAYAL

Up in here where the air is clean.

There are pandas that wear armor and they are mean.

They'll yell your name and when you look.

They'll sock you with a big right hook.

Don't mess with them.

Don't even try.

Because those fuzzy little pandas will make you cry.

THE REAL YOU

You can take solace.

In the fact that I did notice.

Your new hair and clothes.

And what you did to your nose.

But I liked you the way you were.

Before you changed yourself to what others prefer.

Go back to the one I knew.

The one a criticism would eschew.

You had everything you should want.

Forget about miserable people compelled to taunt.

SILKY-SMOOTH

A selfish shellfish.

Only looking out for his own.

Will steal anything.

Even if it's only a bone.

Chased by the cops.

He crawled with all his might.

Wishing he was born with the gift of flight.

He ended up in a seaside jail.

No money for bail.

Stared out at his home all day long.

Knowing he had to stay strong.

Waves crashed up against his cell.

No escaping was what he could tell.

One day he got out.

And leaped into the sea.

Went back to school and got a law degree.

FREE-FLOW

Take a stroll.

Through a crowded park.

See the faces.

In the light, not dark.

Exchange a smile.

Share a nod.

Throw a dirt clod.

Rent a boat.

Fling a Frisbee.

Live for sunny days.

As it busts through the haze.

Lay down in the grass.

Take a nap.

Let happiness fill in the gap.

Don't worry about what is slanted.

Never take any of it for granted.

BEACH DAYS HAZE

The sand is soft.

The waves are cold and massive.

White clouds hover just above the swells.

A pelican dive-bombs a surfer just for laughs.

A beach ball gets popped by an umbrella.

The sun bakes a tourist to a fire engine's red.

A baby chases perturbed seagulls.

You pull into a shore break tube and get slammed.

A perfect day at the beach.

There is no substitute.

THE PRO

The even keel.

Nerves made of steel.

Never too high or too low.

Reap the rewards that you sow.

Keep it all in check.

Play your cards above deck.

They'll figure you out soon.

Then you're doomed.

TREASURES

A long goodbye.

A short hello.

A sweat that makes your forehead glow.

A slick sidewalk.

A dessert feast.

Unafraid to fuel the beast.

A panic attack.

A memory you want back.

A lost love.

A found friend.

The most magical day you don't want to end.

THE TRANSPARENT PERSON

The know it all.

From down the hall.

Got his knowledge at the mall.

Ask him a question and he will stall.

Because it's all an act.

He doesn't know anything for fact.

A pretender is all he is.

Nothing but myths is all he gives.

We can all do without.

His presence brings no clout.

He's simply a ruse.

Don't let him become your muse.

IMPERFECT SURPRISES

A jagged edge that protrudes from the west.

A perfectly made up bed for an uninvited guest.

An undercooked meal.

An obnoxious seal.

Planning things too far in advance.

A waste of time to take the chance.

Meeting somebody unique.

Working out your obliques.

All for not?

Take an early afternoon nap on a cot.

Letting your brain rot.

Inducing creative thoughts out of a bland person.

Getting into life with total immersion.

PAYBACK

A rickety chair.

That just don't care.

Came over this afternoon.

Acting like a goon.

Threw a punch.

Missed by that much.

Chucked him the fire

Because he drew my ire.

MINI-THUG

The little manipulator.

Gets everything he wants.

Goes around throwing taunts.

Never feels what they do.

Stealing peoples' candy for him to chew.

Why can't he just grow up?

Stop with all the theatrics and fits!

Go play in the snow, put on some mitts!

Let go of the anger and bask in the glory.

That would be a nice twist to the story.

CRY-BYE

The pain kicks you in the gut.

Why can't she just stay?

Why does it have to be this way?

If she leaves, what good will it do?

Who will you talk to?

There's no hope.

It's like holding onto an already cut rope.

Pray that her pain isn't so bad.

It'll take years of being sad.

Hate to see her go.

I had so much love still to show.

MIDNIGHT MIND MOVIE

Cold stone cracks underfoot.

Trying to get your reputation to take root.

A crowded street.

A lonely corner.

Being neglected while trying to place an order.

A group hug.

A trench you dug.

A bikini-wearing poodle with no water in sight.

A selfish psychologist who cares nothing of your plight.

A chocolate sundae treat on a sunny afternoon.

A friend who can't stop acting like a goon.

An exchange of a smile.

A dry kiss under the stars.

Waiting for that taxi to take you to Mars.

A curling wave.

A cracked bat.

A dreamy place you wish you could be at.

ADULTHOOD

Walking along the beach.

All my dreams seem within reach.

Aiming for the stars.

Going after it all.

Not thinking of taking the fall.

When you're young it all seems so close.

Until reality throws its own dose.

Dragging you back down to earth.

Shattering what you thought was reachable.

Stuffing you in your place.

Get ready to join the rat race.

THE CONVERSATIONAL MISFIT

Don't visit for too long.

Your conversation leaves too much to be desired.

A speechwriter you should have hired.

I can only listen shortly before I go nuts.

Your stories remind me of a klutz.

Please get better at talking.

Or you'll always just see me walking.

LUNCHBREAK FOLLY

Gently waltzing into work.

I can't wait to see my boss, the jerk.

Another nine hours I will grind away.

While trust fund baby's play in the hay.

Why can't I win the lottery?

Spend my days making pottery?

Can't wait for my lunch break.

With a friend I will take.

We'll talk about our dreams and goals!

Of buying a sailboat that runs on coal.

We'll daydream aloud until our boss gives us a shout.

"Get back to work and make me money!"

...Don't ever refer to me as Sonny.

ANXIOUS MOMENT

A scowl...

Blood boiling...

Fists clenched...

Teeth grinding...

Sweat beads...

A stomach tied in knots...

Pressure...

Let it go!

The attainable heights you will know.

GLORY HOG

Waves buttering up to the reef below.

Fish arguing over who goes first.

A crab crawling upside down along the boardwalk.

Drawing attention to oneself.

Do it while you can.

FLATSPELL

The ocean is flat.

Where's everybody at?

They're sipping coffee waiting for the next swell.

Until then everything is not so well.

With no waves there is no fun.

Just sitting around waiting for the flatness to get done.

Some will go to work.

Some will sleep.

There are no great tube rides to reap.

It's depressing and sad.

When the swell hits we'll all be glad.

Get back into the sea where we belong.

Because watching a waveless ocean is just wrong.

MUCH TO DO ABOUT YOU!

The celebratory cheers from your fans echo through the room.

There is no need for doom and gloom.

They came to see you.

To witness your feat.

Being idolized is actually pretty neat.

It doesn't happen to everyone.

Enjoy it while it lasts.

Because hero worship only comes in fleeting blasts.

NEVER QUIT

The message received was forgotten.

He crept out into the cold undressed.

He stumbled to a broken pay phone.

And laid his body to rest.

The ice cold pavement felt good.

Despite his body aches.

He craved blueberry pancakes.

Morning came and the bright sun rose.

The paramedics took him out of those clothes.

He was gifted another day.

Just had to convince himself that things would be okay.

EARLY BIRD

An untold truth...

A savvy sleuth...

A pulled hamstring...

A doorbell you ring...

Running through the bright white snow...

With nowhere in particular to go...

A chocolate sundae on a cold afternoon...

Coming back to see you soon...

Holidays with many friends...

Regretting that it always ends...

Finding love in the unlikeliest of places...

Trying to remember all those faces...

Stopping to simplify the most complicated of things...

Waking up to the same old bird who sings.

ISOLATED ARROGANCE

He smiles broadly and lets it sink it.

It always feels good to win!

He pounds his chest.

And pumps his fist!

We all get the gist...

An egomaniac to its fullest degree.

Has time for only me.

In the end he'll be alone.

Nobody will tolerate his evil bone.

So a winner on the field he definitely is.

Alone everywhere else is all his.

SUBLIMINAL CURRENTS

The non-verbal cues.

Painting in all different hues.

Sweeping views.

A soft touch on the arm.

A sudden motion that causes alarm.

A long hug.

An emotional drug.

Tip-toeing back to sleep.

A dream you wish you could keep.

Riding a stubborn horse.

Forgetting her birthday...of course!

Not looking back.

Never buying off the rack.

Settling on an honest day's pay.

Sometimes even getting your way.

STUD

Oozing with confidence.

His decisions make no sense.

He won't listen to reason.

Would consider it treason.

He's got it all figured out.

Headed to the next level with plenty of clout.

Why take advice from those who know?

When you've got nowhere but up to go.

STANDARDS

The sanctity of the conversation must be preserved.

Good lines of dialogue required and served.

No room for ignorant banter.

No time for useless talk.

If you don't have something entertaining to say.

Take a walk!

DESPERATION UNDONE

The deer trudges through the snow.

Where his boots went he does not know.

Passes by stores but has no cash.

Wants to run in, steal something and dash.

But he would stick out too much.

Everybody would know his game.

Sometimes being an animal in a peoples' world is pretty lame.

UNDER THE RADAR

What defines brilliance, we do not know.

Is it somebody who doesn't have far to go?

Or do we listen to rhetoric then cast a vote?

Is it the guy who can talk to a goat?

Or the girl who swims through the moat?

How about the thug with the tattoo on his throat?

Or the quiet intellect who refuses to gloat?

Or maybe, just maybe, it's the eccentric who built the concrete boat.

FAKER

He stepped to the podium with so much to say.

Had been sweating nervously for this special day.

It was all ready to go; his head was clear.

Then he heard somebody sneer.

Suddenly he wished the exit was near.

But it wasn't, he had a long way to go.

He dreamt that somebody else would tell them so.

That they all paid good money to hear him speak.

Stories he told to a similar group last week.

He wasn't a fraud.

But he wasn't as true to form as they thought.

Felt originality was over-wrought.

So he pushed through and repeated himself one more painstaking time.

To have to listen to him again would be considered a crime.

TELL-TALE CLUE

The hub of trouble lies within the eyes.

You can tell by looking deep into them if they act as spies.

Let your eyes tell the truth.

Allow them to let others in.

You won't be doubted.

They'll help you win.

Because nobody wants to figure out a schemer.

They'd rather be friends with an honest dreamer.

TRAPPED

A turtle shuffles to work through the dense fog...

Thinking of giving up everything he's worked for to start a blog...

To write about his lifethe first hundred years...

Listening to his dreams always brings him to tears...

He sheds his sunglasses and wipes the water...

Wishes the women around him were hotter...

He opens the door to his office...

And sips at his cold coffee...

Sits down to make a cold call to someone he actually might like in-person...

Nothing like living in a cubicle...

Working life in total immersion...

INSPECTION DECEPTION

Why do we look so closely?

Does it really help?

Just get the broad strokes.

Forget the details.

When it gets too complex.

It always derails.

Kick back and enjoy the ride.

Let the problems just slide.

OOPS

When his ship came in.

He offered a grin.

A sought after tin.

It was a gift from a lost love.

The ring fit his finger like a glove.

He stared at it night and day.

Wishing some luck would come his way.

She finally showed up one day.

She looked nothing like he thought.

He became distraught.

She resented his mood.

All he did was sit around all day and brood.

They parted company in good measure.

He boarded the ship in search of a new treasure.

ADVENTURES

Can you see through the mist?

Do you get the gist?

It's not always what you think.

Put down that silly drink!

Where will you go next?

Jump a train headed west.

Get to the beach and get tubed.

Head to the mountains and ride a snow-covered wave.

Have coffee with an old friend on a windy porch.

Call your family to let them know you've found it.

And can't wait to expound it.

YOUTH

The kids in play.

Should have all day.

To bounce around.

Play uninhibited in the sun.

Don't worry about anything but having fun.

Stay young for as long as you can.

No need to rush becoming a man.

CHERISHABLE GOODS

If you should leave too early.

Don't forget what we had.

It wasn't nearly that bad.

Good times will always come and go.

The fondest memories are what you should know.

RELUCTANT LIMELIGHT

The last thing he wanted.

Was to be taunted.

He worked so hard all week.

The outlook did not look bleak.

But when he strode onto the pitch.

The last thing he felt was rich.

He waved to the fans with a fake smile.

But wanted to get out of there.

Run for at least a mile.

But with the microscope on you

There's no going back.

Sooner or later they'll realize that all you are is a hack.

AGING OUT

Growing old has its perks.

Have way less time for inconsiderate jerks.

You can forget things and not get hit.

Someone will always grab a chair for you to sit.

When were the good ol' days?

Where did they go?

The best times you will ever know.

All gone.

Never to return.

Don't go back to it.

It will only burn.

AWKWARD GLANCES

She lacked quality and class.

Walked away after she broke the glass.

Left him sitting there in his drink.

With plenty of time to think.

He went wrong at the first look.

Never should have put down that book.

But he got drawn in like they all do.

Would have been better off with eyesight like Mr. Magoo!

Now it all hurts.

The time never feels right.

His outlook filled with blight.

Go home.

Go to sleep.

Get up and forget it all.

Hopefully you won't see her walking down the hall.

THE PROCLAMATION

The train rolls lazily into the station.

Seems like an eternity he's been waitin'.

She steps into his sight.

The tears he must fight.

He hasn't seen her in years.

Realizes he can rest his fears.

She smiles brightly and runs his way.

This is the day!

They embrace on the platform in front of the crowd.

And proclaim their love for each other out loud.

They receive a round of applause.

And are so proud that they stuck with the cause.

Special feelings are rare.

It's spring...must be love in the air!

DWELLING

Thinking too much about a certain thought.

Can make your brain start to rot.

Let go of it when it's over.

Go pick a four-leaf clover.

Getting hung up on the negative doesn't help.

It'll cause you to yelp.

Forget about the past.

Go out and have a blast!

SICK DAY

Quiet comfort slips into the room.

Resting her head on a soft pillow.

Soft music lulls her to sleep.

The happy dreams tonight she wishes she could keep.

A new morning will bring with it new hope.

A bright sun.

A talkative bird at dawn.

An alarm clock that fails to work.

Sleeping in undetected.

Calling in sick and watching the day go by.

Words to live by.

INSULTING INQUIRIES

The existentialism bores the common man.

What is there beyond?

What if we're all not really here?

Is there a point to speculate that which you hold dear?

Don't bother living what you can't.

Seize the now.

Enjoy yourself today.

There should be no other way.

Don't overthink it.

Never overdrink it.

It wasn't meant to analyze.

It's not a specimen.

The world is here to be your joy.

Don't make it a debatable headache.

CONCENTRATION

Using special words is absurd...

There is beauty in simplicity that we can all enjoy...

Go make an unmovable toy...

Stare at it all day and see what it does...

NO HIGH SEAS FOR ME

Why me?

I don't want to go to sea.

I might get sick.

Or left alone.

Certainly can't order a scone.

Life on the high seas can't be that fun.

Got a ton of laundry to be done.

Where's my remote?

How about my phone?

Like this I will continue to drone.

There's probably somebody else more prone.

Leave me on land.

Let me do what I do.

Here, take my shoe.

ME TARGET

You think you're smart?

Reinvent the dart.

Draw it on the computer.

Make it 3D.

Throw it at a virtual board.

That has a picture of me.

OBSCURED CONSCIOUSNESS

Odd angles.

Hit the shadows.

No need to go into battle.

Simmering heat

Creates water boiling on a rusted stove.

The snow falls heavily onto a caved-in roof.

A tired farmer stokes a fire.

A fat goat steals the best spot in front of the television

And he does not apologize for his selfishness.

A frog in a tattered coat waits patiently at the front door.

Another night in paradise it is.

He knows the frog will come through the window soon and drink all the
tea.

PARTY CRASHER

The train rolls into the station

Now what are we going to do?

After you show up uninvited...

I do have other friends ya know...

We had plenty of places to go...

Until you got here...

Now we'll just stay...

And waste away our days...

At least until you leave.

AN OASIS

A proven theory by chance.

An opportunity to dance

With your lifelong crush.

Don't be in a rush.

You'll find out she's just an illusion.

Pardon the intrusion.

You talk all night about nothing original.

She quotes talk shows.

While you wish yourself away.

Why couldn't the illusion last all day?

Reality sets in and she wasn't nearly as amusing.

Ego doesn't need any bruising.

Call your buddies and go cruising.

Let her drift to the back of your mind.

Get back to the weekly grind.

HORROR SHOW

My dreams are so vivid.

Sometimes they make me livid.

Imagining work situations when I should be calm.

Wish I could dream of chores being gone.

The colors pounce.

The voices muffle.

My feelings and emotions sometimes ruffle.

I wake up in a sweat.

Can't tell if I'm awake yet.

Walk around the house lonely for a while.

Go back to sleep.

Hope for a smile.

My theatre of dreams should entertain me.

Not drain me.

OVERBEARING

Patience matters less when you're not in a hurry.

Pick up that jacket!

We need to scurry.

To an event neither of us cares about.

Hang out with boring bears.

Cracked surfboards hang on the racks.

Bears are too lazy to carry them on their backs.

Don't get too close or they'll smack your face.

Hit fifth gear and get on with the race.

They have four feet.

You have two.

There's way more work for you to do.

Trip and you're done.

What happens next isn't fun.

Lay down.

Wait for the rising sun.

He's gone back to hibernate with his friends.

You always knew his concentration would end.

DEFIANCE

Grazing lazily on dried out hay.

Waiting for the music to play.

Wanna get my groove on.

Let it all go.

Have people take pictures of my moves...so slow.

Who says I can't dance?

I want them to bring it.

Together we can sing it.

HATA

The answer is there.

But you don't care.

Because then the drama would go.

And everybody would know.

That you're made of fluff.

Your chest you will puff.

Why can't despair leave your brain?

Isn't happiness something you would like to attain?

This is wrong!

That isn't right!

You always get the slight.

That isn't always true.

Maybe it's because of you.

And the way you look at things.

Time to enjoy what life brings.

Before it's too late.

Let go of the hate.

THE SPENDER

A child counts his savings.

Can't wait to quench his cravings.

To the store he will go.

All he will want is more.

Up and down the aisles.

Wanting everything in sight.

He isn't rich.

And thus, his plight.

Wanting it all.

But taking less.

When he can afford everything.

Is anyone's guess.

For today is about a simple toy.

One that will bring him years of joy.

He will settle for it and be content.

It's much healthier than being all bent.

KEEP MOVING

I've turned old

Now what do I do?

I've got dreams to live.

People to scold.

Stories to tell.

Places to go.

Exotic locations to know.

A beautiful life to live.

This big heart you gave me to give.

Just hope I have time to do it all.

FEARLESS

A far off place that you imagine daily...

A midday phone call to take you out of your misery...

A letter you open when things couldn't get worse...

A story with a perfect verse...

Finding that ultimate escape...

Walking out to the tip of an iceberg...

Raising your arms in triumph at the bright orange sunset...

Your heart slowing down to a reasonable speed...

Living life to its fullest...

Indeed.

PARTICLES & BARNACLES

Laughter abounds.

Hugs permeate.

No need to ruminate.

Into the sea.

Alone with me.

Forgetting my degree.

To study the habits of sharks.

Not the human ones though.

They're too boring and predictable.

OH YEAH

We chose to meet.

Not worried about being discreet.

In the center square.

Paparazzi beware.

Where are you?

I'm right here.

Next to the scarf-wearing deer.

Sit down for coffee.

Wash it down with toffee.

Run to the limo.

A weekend getaway to go to.

Tickets all paid.

Can't wait to get weighed.

INGENUITY

If you're not so sure.

Please demure.

If you know it all.

Go talk to the guy down the hall.

If silence bores you.

Remember that people will choose to ignore you.

If it's all too much.

Let's go out...but only Dutch.

Pleasure...pain?

Just choose a lane.

THE CHASE

The world comes at you.

Like a speeding race car that just lost a tire.

Turn for one second and it smacks you in the face.

Run from it.

But it will always catch up to you.

Hide all you want.

It knows where you are.

Avoid it?

It just keeps calling like a jilted girlfriend who fell too in love with your humor.

Accept it.

Love it.

It's only here once.

Go for it all.

Not in one day though.

Spread out the passion over a century.

If you're lucky enough.

FLIMSY FIELD TRIP

Cheer for the underdog

Let up on the champ.

Morning is getting damp.

Throw our sleeping bags in the truck.

Along with all the other junk.

Off to the game is where we're headed.

Finding tickets.

Something we dreaded.

Friends along with us.

People watching and eating.

Day off!

Full of treating.

Dance under the stars after everyone leaves.

Get home after curfew and get busted again.

SIESTA

Starting anew.

With things to do.

A workout.

A lunch.

Cups of coffee on a patio sheltering the rain.

A break-up that causes immense pain.

Work that drives you insane.

Too much in your brain.

A meditation too short.

A girl to court.

Dancing until dawn with your dream.

Watching the steam

Seep out the seam.

CHILL OUT BRO

I forgot to call.

So sue me!

I was busy having fun.

No need to listen to you complain.

From that I choose to abstain.

Why are you so negative?

Just chill-out.

Hanging loose is what it's all about.

HOOKED

The promise of dreams brings us here.

To go for things we hold so dear.

We'll listen to the cheer.

Then put our lives in gear.

At least for a week.

Then we'll go back to being weak.

Can't sustain the grind.

Leave what we really came here for behind.

Go out to the lake and throw in the line.

Catch a fish whose day is no longer fine.

Spontaneously combust into thin air.

It's a little too late to care.

UNDERAPPRECIATED MELTDOWN

A daunting task is such.

Only if you make it too much.

I came to you for advice.

You wouldn't even put down your vice.

We sat and talked under the stars.

Covered topics from here to Mars.

Sipping expensive drinks.

Under the impression that they'll help us think.

But all it did was rile you up.

That's when you threw your cup.

And got us kicked out.

Now what do we do?

Do you know of someplace new?

A hideout with a beautiful waitress.

And not too much light.

Something to eat.

A little respite.

For good conversation is hard to find.

But never you mind.

CRAMPED THOUGHTS

A dream of mine made me sad...

That I couldn't be glad...

That I missed the game-winning goal...

And had to escape through a diagonal hole...

Into another dimension where all was spotted...

The contract I signed was never dotted...

I want out!

I no longer want to play!

Don't want to stay!

This isn't what I thought it was about...

Should be better...

I have more clout...

Get me a burger and some fries...

Throw out all the lies...

Enough with everyone wearing ties!

Just give me my goal...

And then I'll go to work...

Back to being a daytime clerk.

THE JOKE IS ON YOU

Seals dance to an underwater beat.

Played by a blowfish DJ who ate too much for breakfast.

Dolphins try to crash the party.

But are turned away.

A cruise ship creates a massive wake.

The dolphins get barreled until they find another party.

A BBQ hosted by lobsters.

The irony is striking.

The main course is crab.

They showed up late.

And didn't know not to stay.

Everyone laughs.

Except the crabs.

Who wished they'd stayed at bingo.

PSYCHE

What do we have in common?

Not much you say?

We both breathe.

And have two eyes.

And walk upright.

And speak with our mouths.

Ha!

Gotcha!

When we going out?

Never?

Despite having all that in common?

Your expectations seem too high anyway.

GRINDER

When the clock strikes ten.

You know it must end.

Get up and get out.

Working for the man is what it's all about.

Don't dream too much.

It will only hurt.

Make your life seem like dirt.

HIGH MAINTENANCE

The knight rides in to assist.

The damsel says no...

What a dis!

Why can't it be simple?

Why can't she be nice?

Why can't a daring rescue suffice?

SOURMAN

Speeding around at the sound of light.

Can't figure out when his life took flight.

But all is good now.

There is no grief.

His goals won't be stolen by a pessimistic thief.

The sun shines.

The flowers bloom.

No room in his life for doom and gloom.

A part of him was awakened.

To a long time.

For goodness saken.

He smiles sincerely.

The bitterness no more.

Positivity abounds galore.

ALARM CLOCK WELCOME

A bird up early before the rest.

Trying to keep quiet.

Doing his best.

But the sun is up.

The day has begun.

Let's get going.

Have some fun.

He keeps the epic morning to himself for just a split.

Then he starts yelling.

It's all legit.

Even if it frazzles your neighbors a bit.

VAROOOM!!!

Racing cars.

Jumping bumps.

Those drivers sure take their lumps.

Making quick decisions.

Defying death.

Sometimes holding their breath.

Roaring into the pits.

Getting instructions in little, static-filled bits.

Going round and round until somebody wins.

Their lives should be titled...

As the world spins.

JUST LET ME SLEEP

The headache feels like a thousand foot wave.

Crashing through my head.

Crickets signing in stereo.

Bringing on the dread.

Please tell me it's Saturday.

I need this day off.

If it's a work day I might just scoff.

Or call in sick.

The thoughts are so heavy.

They make me sick.

When are the holidays?

When do we exchange gifts?

Ready to holler!

Shoes need some lifts.

There goes that alarm clock again.

I must be headed to work.

Checking paperwork all day with Captain Kirk.

THE WORKHORSE

The donkey paves a path through sanity.

He knows who has lied to him.

Who hasn't paid their bills.

Might buck them off.

Cheap thrills.

They pack his back full of their stuff.

No need to get rough.

He'll get you there.

Just don't rush him.

This is his job.

He's not escaping it like you.

Believe him, he'd have plenty else to do.

PENNILESS THOUGHTS

Up a creek.

Without a paddle.

Friends will tattle.

They'll tell what you've done.

The times you'll get busted.

For having too much fun.

Always end up on the run.

Try to calm down.

Lay in the sun.

Tie your hair in a bun.

Talk to the back-scratching monkey wrench.

You can find him on the titled park bench.

He offers good advice.

But you pay a fee.

A clearer life he'll help you see.

MORNING BRILLIANCE

The streetlights shimmer through the fog.

You go walking by with your dog.

It beats the midday oppressive smog.

Your two legs and his four.

He gets tired easily.

Short stubby legs get sore.

Sipping a coffee.

Nodding to strangers.

Being up too early.

The only danger.

Then she strolls around the corner.

Your heart skips its usual beat.

Her dog jogs over to you.

And lays claim to your feet.

Her smile outshines the not yet risen sun.

You know that she is the one.

CHARACTER BUILDERS

A paper cut that bums you out.

A punch to the face

Right in your snout.

A pulled muscle.

A hampered hamstring.

A kick to the shin.

Leaves a ding.

A slap to the arm.

A bite to the ear.

All the knocks that you hold dear.

Play it enough and you'll pay the price.

Our bodies weren't mean to be all clean and nice.

IS IT YOU?

The world needs leaders.

Voracious readers.

Those who acquire knowledge and share it.

Invents things.

Dare it.

Sitting back and doing nothing is the crime.

The world needs you now!

There isn't a whole lot of time.

Step up and make an impact.

No need to redact.

Just go for it.

Make it right.

Get your sleep in the middle of the night.

We have to leave something for the kids to follow.

Otherwise all they will do is wallow.

FREELOADERS

Dogs come home from a walk...

So excited they'll eat chalk...

Running full speed through the trail...

They'll keep going right through the hail...

It's the highlight of their day...

Don't have jobs...

Don't have pay...

Come home and eat...

Go fast asleep...

Plenty more good times to reap...

I don't blame them...

But I do resent...

All my money they unlawfully spent...

CHIN UP

A cracked coin.

A pulled groin.

A run that makes you sick.

I love that makes you tick.

Dreams that make you go.

Affection you will show.

Live well.

Work hard.

BBQ in your backyard.

Believe in yourself.

Offer help.

Always look up.

Don't hang your head.

This life you should not dread.

FAMILY

A meteoritic rise to fame.

Totally committed to playing the game.

It'll eat you up if you aren't ready.

Tricks can become pretty heady.

Don't lose yourself in the hype.

Keep talking to your lifelong friends all night.

Stay grounded.

Don't get hounded.

It might all come to pass.

Leaving you feeling kind of crass.

No money to fill your tank up with gas.

Keep your family close.

They'll always love you the most.

MOATED

A little boat.

That drifts around in the moat.

The kids come to play.

The boat wishes they could stay.

But at dusk they leave.

And the boat will heave.

On the waves that the ducks make.

Stop moving for Pete's sake!

You can't ski in my wake.

Go out to the sea.

Leave the moat all to me.

THE SEARCH

The alter ego.

More harm than good?

Who sets his mood?

Doing what you do?

Or quite the opposite?

Living your dreams?

Or repeating nightmarish themes?

Listening to your heart?

Or blindly moving on random wave lengths of thought?

Making more of you than you're not.

Better get a hold of him.

Before he does you in.

BLAND LAND

Brains wasted.

Food not tasted.

Traveling at the speed of light.

Afraid to take flight.

Head down in the ground.

Not reaching for the clouds.

Potential left untapped.

Following the life the corporations mapped.

Need to find your inner gift.

And share it.

Because it's there.

It just won't text you to let you know where.

INQUISITIVE CONGESTION

A change in seasons.

A plethora of reasons.

Snow blanketing the landscape.

Leaves cracked to pieces.

Conflict never ceases.

Find your own hideout.

Where your mind can take a nap.

Avoid the clutter trap.

Easy come.

Easy go.

There is still so much to know.

QUIRKY FRIEND

Innocuous melodies whistle through town.

Here comes that little car all stuffed up with the clown.

He's ready to make you laugh and giggle.

Do a wiggle.

He's always in a good mood.

Never brood.

Why you so happy Mr. Clown?

I want to see you just for once frown.

Are you a fake?

Are you really that happy?

As I get older I find your jokes sort of sappy.

DELIGHTFUL MELODY

The mysteries of life.

Will never be found.

Otherwise, there would be nobody around.

We'd figure it all out.

And make a bigger mess than we should.

Instead of just concentrating on doing good.

Your life.

Your brain.

Your mission.

Helping out is what we're all wishing.

Too much sadness.

Overloads of worry.

Slow down.

Don't scurry.

Smile and relax.

Play the sax.

Listen to life's song.

You can never go wrong.

TIMELESS SCENES

Scuba gear for a land-locked surfer.

Playing tennis with the girl of your dreams.

Losing graciously.

Scoring a hot stock tip from a stranger over coffee.

Doodling on your notebook.

Throwing your cell phone into the river.

Freedom.

Eating a sandwich along the shore.

Playing basketball on your way home from a long day.

Skipping a meeting to go to a midday ballgame.

Talking for uninterrupted hours with your favorite friend.

Summertime.

Don't let it end.

UNIVERSAL LOVE

There are things much bigger than us.

Don't be afraid to trust.

Go for it.

You won't be a bust.

Believe it in your heart.

Chase it with your gut.

Do not let yourself get into a rut.

Take it by the horns.

Live it full.

Being positive is oh, so cool.

Dress yourself in wool.

Stand up on a stool.

Proclaim your love of life.

FROM DURDEN

Jealously and rage.

People locked in a cage.

Sadness, madness, hate, and anger.

Deceit and dishonesty.

Let it all go!

There is so much more to know.

Love and compassion.

Friendship and laughs.

Don't stress about the gaffs.

Slow down!

Walk with purpose.

We all deserve this.

Think about what you really do.

And how other people help you.

Return the favors.

Live with patience.

Life is what we make this.

Don't get caught up in all the hubs.

Stop once in a while.

And enjoy the belly rubs.

ACKNOWLEDGEMENTS

I'd like to thank all of the people who are in my life and also those who have come in and out of it. You are my inspiration and motivation. Special thanks to my wife and son, dad, sister and uncle and all the Casey families back east. Also, thanks to the DRS Family, you rock! I appreciate all your love, support and patience.

ABOUT THE AUTHOR

MARK VINCENT LINCIR writes daily at his blog
markvincentlincir.com and is a featured columnist at Soccer365.com. His
work has also been featured at Goal.com and in Manchester United's
Matchday Programme. His first book, **A SOCCER LIFE IN SHORTS** is
available at amazon.com.